My Life
My Words

A memoir in progress

Thanks to:

The Birren Center for Guided Autobiography for inspiration throughout.

Daphne Foulkes-Jones for family history writing tips.

Bree Gillis, Breeze Designz for design of this journal.

Copyright Mali Bain, 2023

Table of Contents

- **PREFACE** — 3
- **INTRODUCTION** — 5
  - About NextGen Story: Custom Publishing — 9
- **PART 1: TOOLS TO GET YOU STARTED** — 11
  - A Few Notes on Writing — 13
  - Clarify Your Book's Purpose — 17
  - Narrow Your Focus — 21
  - Guided Writing: One Memory — 30
  - Guided Writing: To a child — 40
- **PART 2: FAMILY HERITAGE** — 45
  - Your Heritage - Maternal Side — 47
  - Your Heritage - Paternal Side — 63

PART 3: LIFE STORY QUESTIONS — 71

Brief Biography — 73
Turning Points — 83
Childhood — 95
Youth — 111
Work — 119
Love — 123
Cultural — 127
Family Ties — 139
Parenting — 145
Perspective — 153

CONCLUSION — 163

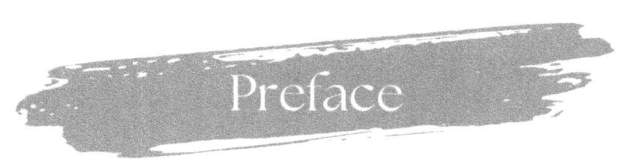

Preface

Welcome, glad you're here!

You have this book in your hands; therefore you or someone you know sees the value of sharing your life story. This is wonderful news.

Before you begin, though - why take the time to write your own life story?

Writing your life story is a chance to reflect on your experiences, lessons, and personal growth. The insights and realizations you share can inspire and guide others. If you choose to share more broadly, your life story becomes a part of our shared human history, offering insights into different perspectives.

Documenting your story on paper preserves your story as a part of your family's history - both for those whom you know but who may not know the 'whole story' - and for generations to come.

Writing your story is truly a gift that keeps on giving - to you and to others, for generations to come.

Mali Bain, November 2023

"Preserve your memories, keep them well. What you forget, you can never retell."

-Louisa May Alcot

Introduction

This journal will support you to take on one of the most meaningful, rewarding and challenging tasks of your life: recording your own life story.

The process of writing about and reflection on one's life in itself can provide insight, joy, and healing.

Some may also choose to use this journal as the starting place for compiling a memoir or life story book. Creating a life story book - whether for family or 'public' is a beautiful way to share your stories, experiences, and legacy.

Either way, capturing your memories on paper is a meaningful way to share your memories, traditions and values with generations to come.

There are a few features of this journal intended to support you in your writing.

- **Questions to consider:** In each section you will find a list of questions to consider. Consider each of these a 'spark' rather than a homework assignment. It is completely natural for a question about your siblings to remind you of your parents, or of a holiday, for example. Write the memories that come to mind, whether or not they directly relate to the question at the top of the page.

- **Blank pages:** You will find, as you begin to reminisce, that memories come in 'no particular order'. Write down what comes up as it arises - make use of the blank pages for this purpose. You can put the content in some sort of meaningful order later, if you choose: for now, it's about capturing the memories.

- **Boxes - and 'beyond the box'**: Yes, you will see boxes in a few of the sections. Your life will likely not neatly fit into the categories and boxes in this book. That's a good thing: that's what makes your life unique, interesting to others, and relatable. This is your journal, your memoir in progress: feel free to simply cross out a title, adjust the wording as you see fit, or add your own additional content on the blank pages.

This is your journal - and it's up to you to decide how to use it. You may prefer to work through each page in order - or, you may prefer to flip to a page & work with the question that's there.

If you're looking for a place to begin, here are my top three recommendations:

- **Clarify Your Purpose & Narrow Your Focus:** If you are considering publishing your writing into a book, eventually - start with these sections.

- **Brief Biography:** Sometimes it helps to start with 'just the facts' before delving into the details: if you're one of those people, start here.

- **Turning Points**: Wanting to get to the really significant bits - the parts of your life where you really stood at a crossroads and chose which way to go? Then start here to get the wheels turning...

Whatever order you approach these questions, and however you record your answers, I hope this journal support your continued recording of **your words** about **your life**. This is, indeed, your greatest legacy.

"Your story
is the greatest legacy
that you will leave to your friends.
It's the longest-lasting legacy
you will leave to your heirs."

- Steve Saint

About NextGen Story: Custom Publishing

NextGen Story: Custom Publishing is a custom life story and family history publishing service.

I began NextGen Story because of the work I did supporting my grandmother to compile her life story into a "real book". She loved her book, and her words are a meaningful legacy that will last for generations to come.

Since then, it has been my privilege and honour to help dozens of families create their own life story or family history books.

This life story journal in your hands can, if you choose, begin your journey towards publishing a life story book - for friends, family, or beyond. When you're ready to take the next step, reach out to our team at NextGen Story: Custom Publishing.

And for now - just write, and don't look back!

Mali Bain
Founder, NextGen Story: Custom Publishing
mali@nextgenstory.com
1-800-953-4942

"A book
is a gift
you can open
again
and
again."

- Garrison Keillor

Part 1
Tools to Get You Started

"Abandon the idea
that you are ever going to finish.
Lose track of the 400 pages
and write just one page for each day,
it helps.
Then when it gets finished,
you are always surprised."

— *John Steinbeck*

A Few Notes on Writing

Writing about your own life can be incredibly fun - after all, you're unearthing memories that only you can tell. We've all been told different things at different points: here's a few notes.

Choose a time to write every day: Writing at a certain time each day is a fabulous way to consistently add to your life story journal. If useful, you could make a goal - 20 minutes a day, a page a day, 200 words per day - whatever suits you.

Pop this journal into your bag as you go about your day: jot down an idea that comes to you in the grocery story, or out on a walk, or in a line-up. Then you'll have something to write about when you come to your scheduled time.

This is not about literary process - it's about your life. There is no need to wax poetic or use excessive adjectives - unless of course that is your habitual way of writing/speaking. One place to start can be the "5Ws": What happened, to Whom, Where, When, and Why does this matter? If you are able to share stories at a dinner party, you're able to write: your task is to translate your speaking voice onto paper.

Don't worry about spelling, grammar, or punctuation: all of that can be worked on later. You are the only one who can offer the content - YOUR life story, your words. You can write in sentences, bulleted lists, lines of poetry, or whatever works for you - just write!

Try recording your voice. If you find you don't enjoy writing or typing your memories, what about audio-recordings? You could use either voice-to-text software or the 'dictate' button in Microsoft word. Or, if you'd rather, you could hit 'record' on your cellphone/computer to create an audio version of your stories.

Don't censor your content - yet. There will be parts of your life story that are more challenging to address; areas that you may hesitate to include in an overall life story to be shared. Thinking of your desired reader (see 'narrow your focus'), but without promising that you will ever actually share the content, write out what you'd like to say. This experience can be cathartic and helpful - whether or not you choose to include the content in a book is your own choice

Include what is meaningful to you. As Steve Zouzmer puts it - "meaning is the reason something is worth remembering". Yes, you could describe anything you choose from your past: what you include should be meaningful to you.

Clarify Your Books Purpose
with these 5 Questions

Do you want to get your book completed, printed, and shared with your loved ones (and potentially more)? The most important thing, as you start your book, is to have a crystal-clear purpose. Photos, spelling, layout - all that comes later.

- What is your purpose in creating this book?

  _____
  _____
  _____
  _____
  _____
  _____
  _____
  _____
  _____
  _____

- Why is that purpose important to you?

- Why have you decided to create this book now?

● What 3 things might distract or prevent you from finishing the book?

....

....

....

....

....

....

● How can you address the above factors when they arise?

....

....

....

....

....

....

Narrow Your Focus

Read over the previous questions, and hold on to it: if you're clear on why this book matters, you've set a solid foundation. The next piece is setting the focus or frame for your book.

Intended audience: Who will read the book – family, family & friends, or public? Who is the ONE person you will imagine, as you compile and edit the book? What are they looking for?

Focus: What part of your life will you focus the book on and what is your theme? Consider narrowing in on a particular time period, place, set of experiences, or relationships.

Format: Preparing content for an image-heavy coffee-table book is a different task than writing chapters for a memoir. What will the final product "look" like – memoir, coffee-table book? Approximately how long will the book be?

Content: Whether you are doing your own writing or hiring someone to help, consider many sources of content at the beginning of your project. What content will you include: letters, documents, memorabilia, memories, interviews, genealogical research, photos, and images?

Community: Do you have a support network, whether it be family members or professionals, to help you with the technical aspects of your book project,: editing, custom graphics (maps, family trees), layout, design, and printing?

Guided Writing for Memoir Writers

Welcome to a journey of self-discovery through the power of words. In the following exercises, we'll explore the art of guided writing, each with its unique challenge.

- **One Memory**: invites you to relive a cherished moment, painting it with vivid colors and shapes so others can step into your world. Inspired by Lisa Dale Norton's "Shimmering Images," this exercise will help you unlock the essence of a memory.

- **Writing to a child:** we'll simplify your stories, removing the clutter to share with a young, curious mind. Imagine your child, grandchild, godchild, or grandniece/nephew, listening eagerly and asking, "What happened next?" Keep writing, and let your story captivate their imagination.

GUIDED WRITING: ONE MEMORY

Context: writing in the 1st person about your own memory or experience
Challenge: how do you capture that memory so other people "get it"?

Choose one moment you want to write about
Select a specific memory or moment from your life that holds significance to you.

Tell me the story
Begin by narrating the context surrounding this chosen moment.

What happened?
Elaborate on the events that unfolded during this particular memory.

Who was there?
- Introduce the people or individuals who were present during this memory.

Where were you?
- Describe as much detail as you can remember about the location where this memory took place.

Describe the setting
- Provide details about the environment, such as the time of day, weather, and surroundings.

Describe the smells and the tastes
- Recreate the sensory experience by detailing the scents and flavors associated with this memory.

Find the visuals in your story
- Identify the visual elements in your memory that left a lasting impression.

Describe them with colors and shapes
- Use descriptive language to paint a picture of the visuals in your memory, associating them with colors and shapes.

GUIDED WRITING: TO A CHILD

Context: Writing in the 1st or 3rd person
Challenge: How to simplify the overall story and remove extraneous detail?

Writing in the 1st or 3rd person about your own life
- Think of a grandchild, godchild, or grandniece/nephew. Think of them somewhere between 6 and 12 years old, and tell them the story of "what happened".

Keep the story going
- When you pause, hear their voice asking you, "what happened next?" Keep writing.

How does the story end?
- What do you say at the end of the story? Why?

What was different?
- What was different about your story when told to a child? What did you leave out - and why?

Part 2

Family Heritage

Mother's Family Tree

Great-grandmother	Great-grandmother
Great-grandfather	Great-grandfather
Grandfather	Grandmother

Mother

YOUR HERITAGE- MATERNAL SIDE

Did you ever meet your maternal great-grandparents - your mother's grandparents? If so what do you recall of those interactions?

What do you remember of your maternal grandmother (your mother's mother)?

What do you remember of your maternal grandmother (your mother's mother)?

What do you remember of your maternal grandfather (your mother's father)?

Where were your maternal grandparents born?
Where did they move in their lifetimes?

Where was your mother born?

What stories did your mother tell about her early life and growing-up years?

Describe your mother's siblings. What do you know about his growing-up years and interactions with his siblings?

Was there a particular (maternal) aunt or uncle who was significant in your life? If so, describe them and their role in your life.

Great-grandmother

Great-grandmother

Great-grandfather

Great-grandfather

Grandfather

Grandmother

Father

YOUR HERITAGE- PATERNAL SIDE

Did you ever meet your paternal great-grandparents (your father's grandparents)? If so what do you recall of those interactions?

What do you remember of your paternal grandmother (your father's mother)?

What do you remember of your paternal grandfather (your father's father)?

Where were your paternal grandparents born?
Where did they move in their lifetimes?

Where was your father born?

Describe your father's siblings. What do you know about his growing-up years and interactions with his siblings?

What stories did your father tell about her early life and growing-up years?

Was there a particular (paternal) aunt or uncle who was significant in your life? If so, describe them and their role in your life.

Part 3
Life Story Questions

"A parent or a teacher has only his lifetime; a good book can teach forever"

- Louis L'Amour

Biography

BASIC DETAILS

Full Name: _____

Date of Birth: _____

Place of Birth: _____

EDUCATION

Elementary School: _____

Location: _____

Years: _____

High School: _____

Location: _____

Years: _____

Other: _____

Location: _____

Years: _____

WORK/VOCATION

PLACE   LOCATION   TYPE OF WORK/ROLE

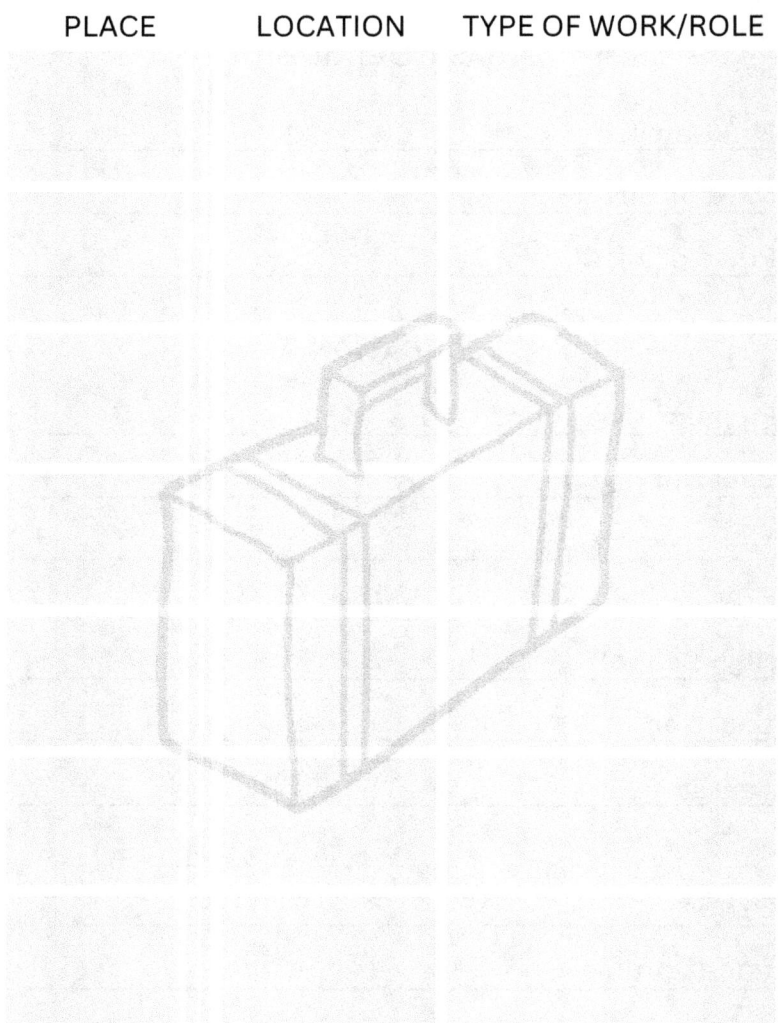

MARRIAGE

Name of Spouse:

Date of Marriage:

Location:

Details:

MARRIAGE

Name of Spouse: _____

Date of Marriage: _____

Location: _____

Details: _____

_____

_____

_____

_____

_____

_____

_____

_____

_____

_____

_____

_____

_____

MARRIAGE

Name of Spouse: _____

Date of Marriage: _____

Location: _____

Details: _____

_____

_____

_____

_____

_____

_____

_____

_____

_____

_____

_____

_____

_____

CHILDREN

NAME   DATE OF BIRTH   LOCATION

SIGNIFICANT LIFE EVENTS

List significant events for a conversation/chapter, like moving, death, building a home, or a major historical event (e.g., WWII) that impacted your life.

Your Life Story: Turning Points

Life is like a winding path, full of twists and turns, and at times, we all reach a crossroads.

These pivotal moments, these branching points, can be life-changing, shaping us into the person we are today. They come in all shapes and sizes, from grand events like weddings and wars, to smaller moments that pack a punch, like stumbling upon a book or taking a hike.

Looking back: what moments in your life have been your branching points? What events left an indelible mark on your path? Which ones nudged you in a new direction?

Take a peek at these questions as they might just unlock a treasure trove of memories and insights into your journey.

Special thanks to Birren Centre for Guided Autobiography for this exercise.

What was the earliest branching point in your life?
- What happened and why was it important? How old were you at the time?

Who influenced your life in a major way?
- Which people were involved with you at the branching points, e.g., family, friends, teachers, doctors, lawyers and others?

Were there any important happenings in your environment, natural or man made crises that changed the direction of your life?

Were there any lucky events in your life that had positive outcomes on the directions it took?
- Such as winning a lottery, getting a new job, or falling in love?

Did your family move their home when you were young?
- What was the impact on you of changing schools, finding new friends?

Have there been any branching points in your life about which you changed your views over time?
- For example, events you were angry about then and contented about now?

Your Life Story: Childhood

Use these questions as inspiration to create content for your life story book. Feel free to modify them or rearrange them as needed to trigger your memories and stories.

How did your parents choose your name? Did you have any other nicknames – if so, how did they come about?

....

....

....

....

....

....

....

....

....

....

What traits did you most admire in your parents? Tell a story from your life that illustrates these traits if you can.

What is your first memory? Describe in as much detail as you can.

Describe your childhood home: which room did you sleep in? What memories do you have of various rooms in the house?

Describe your favourite outdoor play activity as a child.

What was an 'average day' when you were a child: start with waking up in the morning, breakfast, any other morning routines.

What were your favourite possessions as a child - clothing, a particular toy, a bicycle?

What types of technology did you have in your home? What are your memories of early forms of technology (phone/video/etc)

What is the most important life lesson you learned at school?

What were your favourite sports and/or extra-curricular activities?

Who were some of your friends growing up, and how did you pass the time together? Did you have a best friend?

Your Life Story: Youth

Describe yourself as a young adult

Whom did you most admire as a young person?
Whom did you most fear?

Which were your favourite and least favourite subjects in high school?

How did you engage in physical activity and sports?

Did you engage in any hobbies or leisure activities? If so, describe.

What did you want to be when you grew up?

Your Music

As we journey through life, our musical preferences often change and develop. Share some of your cherished songs and favorite music artists below.

Time Frame	Artist	Song

Your Life Story: Work

In general, how do you feel about work and why?

_____

_____

_____

_____

_____

_____

What achievements are you most proud of?

_____

_____

_____

_____

_____

If you had the opportunity to change careers, would you? What would you choose to do instead?

....

....

....

....

....

....

Looking back on your career, is there anything you would have done differently?

....

....

....

....

....

....

Your Life Story: Love

How did you meet your current spouse? How long did you know them before you got married?

....

....

....

....

....

....

....

....

....

....

....

....

What lessons have you learned about love and partnership?

Your Life Story: Cultural

Where were your grandparents on either side born? What significant do those places have in **your** life?

What language(s) have you been exposed to as a child, youth, adult? What have you learned from these other languages/cultures?

What groups, clubs, or organizations have you been a member of? Why did you choose to participate in each?

What role has faith, religion, or spirituality played in your life?

What values are important in your family?

Travels

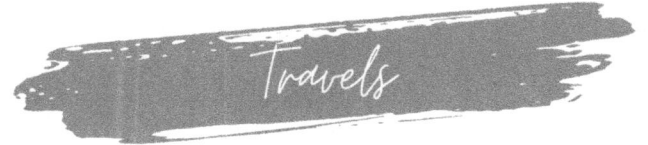

Shade in the countries you've visited below.

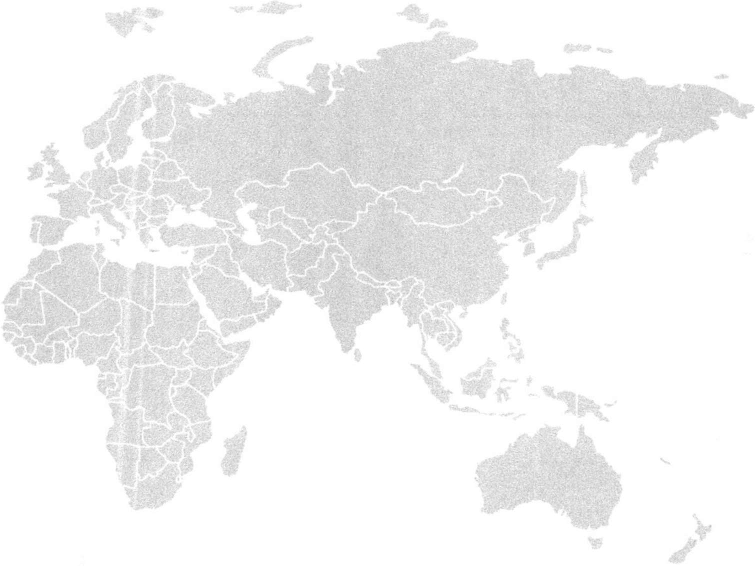

Year	Destination
_____	_____

Year	Destination
_____	_____

Year	Destination
_____	_____

Year	Destination
_____	_____

Year	Destination
_____	_____

FAMILY TIES

How did you get along with your siblings when you were young? Can you tell a story or any memory of your brothers and sisters?

In what ways are you most like your parents? In what ways are you different from them?

Who is/was your favourite relative and why?
Who is/was your least favourite relative and why?

List a few of your most memorable winter holidays

Year

Year

Year

Year

Your Life Story: Parenting

How old were you when you became a parent? In what ways were you ready - what surprised you?

What values do you feel were most important to pass on to your children, and do you think you were successful?

Were you strict or lenient as a parent? Why?

How did your own parents or other role models influence your approach to parenting?

How did parenthood change you?

Your Life Story: Perspective

How would you describe your philosophy of life?

Describe one event or experience that changed the way you thought about the world.

What is the most significant life challenge you have experienced? How did it change your life?

What have you learned about yourself as a result of facing this challenge?

The quote by Benjamin W Decker is "Consider for a moment what you would tell your younger self. This is your legacy." Based on this quote, what advice or message would you give to your younger self, and how would this contribute to your legacy?

Bucket List

A "bucket list" is a compilation of specific experiences, achievements, or places that an individual hopes to accomplish or visit in their lifetime, reflecting their personal goals and dreams. What are some of yours?

- [ ] _____
- [ ] _____
- [ ] _____
- [ ] _____
- [ ] _____

Conclusion

"The only way I can get anything written at all is to write really, really crappy first drafts"
- Anne Lammot,
Award-winning author of 19 books.

Congratulations! You've made it to the end of this small journal and begin to document your life story. As you look back on this journal, take a moment to consider:

What did you most enjoy writing about?

....

....

....

....

What was the most challenging section?

....

....

....

....

"A book is a gift you can open again and again"-
Garrison Keillor

Looking at the sum total of the stories in this little book - what themes, trends, or patterns do you notice?

....

....

....

....

....

....

....

....

....

If you've enjoyed this process - don't stop writing! Keep the regular date you have with yourself - write your memories as they arise. Some of those memories will fit into your first book - others might fit elsewhere.

www.ingramcontent.com/pod-product-compliance
Lightning Source LLC
Chambersburg PA
CBHW070313010526
44107CB00004B/324

* 9 781990 543128 *